Hymns

VOLUME 2

CARA COBBLE TRANTHAM

Study Suggestions

We believe that the Bible is true, trustworthy, and timeless and that it is vitally important for all believers. These study suggestions are intended to help you more effectively study Scripture as you seek to know and love God through His Word.

SUGGESTED STUDY TOOLS

- A Bible
- A double-spaced, printed copy of the Scripture passages that this study covers. You can use a website like *www.biblegateway.com* to copy the text of a passage and print out a double-spaced copy to be able to mark on easily
- A journal to write notes or prayers
- Pens, colored pencils, and highlighters
- A dictionary to look up unfamiliar words

HOW TO USE THIS STUDY

Begin your study time in prayer. Ask God to reveal Himself to you, to help you understand what you are reading, and to transform you with His Word (Psalm 119:18).

Before you read what is written in each day of the study itself, read the assigned passages of Scripture for that day. Use your double-spaced copy to circle, underline, highlight, draw arrows, and mark in any way you would like to help you dig deeper as you work through a passage.

Read the daily written content provided for the current study day.

Answer the questions that appear at the end of each study day.

The inductive method provides tools for deeper and more intentional Bible study. To study the Bible inductively, work through the steps below after reading background information on the book.

1

OBSERVATION & COMPREHENSION
Key question: What does the text say?

After reading the daily Scripture in its entirety at least once, begin working with smaller portions of the Scripture. Read a passage of Scripture repetitively, and then mark the following items in the text:

- Key or repeated words and ideas
- Key themes
- Transition words (Ex: therefore, but, because, if/then, likewise, etc.)
- Lists
- Comparisons and contrasts
- Commands
- Unfamiliar words (look these up in a dictionary)
- Questions you have about the text

2

INTERPRETATION
Key question: What does the text mean?

Once you have annotated the text, work through the following steps to help you interpret its meaning:

- Read the passage in other versions for a better understanding of the text.
- Read cross-references to help interpret Scripture with Scripture.
- Paraphrase or summarize the passage to check for understanding.
- Identify how the text reflects the metanarrative of Scripture, which is the story of creation, fall, redemption, and restoration.
- Read trustworthy commentaries if you need further insight into the meaning of the passage.

3

APPLICATION

Key Question: How should the truth of this passage change me?

Bible study is not merely an intellectual pursuit. The truths about God, ourselves, and the gospel that we discover in Scripture should produce transformation in our hearts and lives. Answer the following questions as you consider what you have learned in your study:

- What attributes of God's character are revealed in the passage?

  Consider places where the text directly states the character of God, as well as how His character is revealed through His words and actions.

- What do I learn about myself in light of who God is?

  Consider how you fall short of God's character, how the text reveals your sin nature, and what it says about your new identity in Christ.

- How should this truth change me?

  A passage of Scripture may contain direct commands telling us what to do or warnings about sins to avoid in order to help us grow in holiness. Other times our application flows out of seeing ourselves in light of God's character. As we pray and reflect on how God is calling us to change in light of His Word, we should be asking questions like, "How should I pray for God to change my heart?" and "What practical steps can I take toward cultivating habits of holiness?"

THE ATTRIBUTES OF GOD

ETERNAL

God has no beginning and no end. He always was, always is, and always will be.

HAB. 1:12 / REV. 1:8 / IS. 41:4

FAITHFUL

God is incapable of anything but fidelity. He is loyally devoted to His plan and purpose.

2 TIM. 2:13 / DEUT. 7:9 / HEB. 10:23

GOOD

God is pure; there is no defilement in Him. He is unable to sin, and all He does is good.

GEN. 1:31 / PS. 34:8 / PS. 107:1

GRACIOUS

God is kind, giving us gifts and benefits we do not deserve.

2 KINGS 13:23 / PS. 145:8 / IS. 30:18

HOLY

God is undefiled and unable to be in the presence of defilement. He is sacred and set-apart.

REV. 4:8 / LEV. 19:2 / HAB. 1:13

INCOMPREHENSIBLE & TRANSCENDENT

God is high above and beyond human understanding. He is unable to be fully known.

PS. 145:3 / IS. 55:8-9 / ROM. 11:33-36

IMMUTABLE

God does not change. He is the same yesterday, today, and tomorrow.

1 SAM. 15:29 / ROM. 11:29 / JAMES 1:17

INFINITE

God is limitless. He exhibits all of His attributes perfectly and boundlessly.

ROM. 11:33-36 / IS. 40:28 / PS. 147:5

JEALOUS

God is desirous of receiving the praise and affection He rightly deserves.

EX. 20:5 / DEUT. 4:23-24 / JOSH. 24:19

JUST

God governs in perfect justice. He acts in accordance with justice. In Him, there is no wrongdoing or dishonesty.

IS. 61:8 / DEUT. 32:4 / PS. 146:7-9

LOVING

God is eternally, enduringly, steadfastly loving and affectionate. He does not forsake or betray His covenant love.

JN. 3:16 / EPH. 2:4-5 / 1 JN. 4:16

MERCIFUL

God is compassionate, withholding from us the wrath that we deserve.

TITUS 3:5 / PS. 25:10
LAM. 3:22-23

OMNIPOTENT

God is all-powerful; His strength is unlimited.

MAT. 19:26 / JOB 42:1-2
JER. 32:27

OMNIPRESENT

God is everywhere; His presencae is near and permeating.

PROV. 15:3 / PS. 139:7-10
JER. 23:23-24

OMNISCIENT

God is all-knowing; there is nothing unknown to Him.

PS. 147:4 / I JN. 3:20
HEB. 4:13

PATIENT

God is long-suffering and enduring. He gives ample opportunity for people to turn toward Him.

ROM. 2:4 / 2 PET. 3:9 / PS. 86:15

SELF-EXISTENT

God was not created but exists by His power alone.

PS. 90:1-2 / JN. 1:4 / JN. 5:26

SELF-SUFFICIENT

God has no needs and depends on nothing, but everything depends on God.

IS. 40:28-31 / ACTS 17:24-25
PHIL. 4:19

SOVEREIGN

God governs over all things; He is in complete control.

COL. 1:17 / PS. 24:1-2
1 CHRON. 29:11-12

TRUTHFUL

God is our measurement of what is fact. By Him we are able to discern true and false.

JN. 3:33 / ROM. 1:25 / JN. 14:6

WISE

God is infinitely knowledgeable and is judicious with His knowledge.

IS. 46:9-10 / IS. 55:9 / PROV. 3:19

WRATHFUL

God stands in opposition to all that is evil. He enacts judgment according to His holiness, righteousness, and justice.

PS. 69:24 / JN. 3:36 / ROM. 1:18

Creation

In the beginning, God created the universe. He made the world and everything in it. He created humans in His own image to be His representatives on the earth.

Fall

The first humans, Adam and Eve, disobeyed God by eating from the fruit of the Tree of Knowledge of Good and Evil. Their disobedience impacted the whole world. The punishment for sin is death, and because of Adam's original sin, all humans are sinful and condemned to death.

Redemption

God sent His Son to become a human and redeem His people. Jesus Christ lived a sinless life but died on the cross to pay the penalty for sin. He resurrected from the dead and ascended into heaven. All who put their faith in Jesus are saved from death and freely receive the gift of eternal life.

Restoration

One day, Jesus Christ will return again and restore all that sin destroyed. He will usher in a new heaven and new earth where all who trust in Him will live eternally with glorified bodies in the presence of God.

Table of Contents

WEEK 1

WEEK 2

WEEK 3

WEEK 4

O Love That Wilt Not Let Me Go

George Matheson, ca. 1882

O Love that will not let me go,
I rest my weary soul in thee;
I give thee back the life I owe,
That in thine ocean depths its flow
May richer, fuller be.

O Light that foll'west all my way,
I yield my flick'ring torch to thee;
My heart restores its borrowed ray,
That in thy sunshine's blaze its day
May brighter, fairer be.

O Joy that seekest me through pain,
I cannot close my heart to thee;
I trace the rainbow through the rain,
And feel the promise is not vain,
That morn shall tearless be.

O Cross that liftest up my head,
I dare not ask to fly from thee;
I lay in dust life's glory dead,
And from the ground there blossoms red
Life that shall endless be.

week 1
day 1

READ:
ROMANS 8:28
PHILIPPIANS 4:8
REVELATION 21:4

O Love That Wilt Not Let Me Go

George Matheson, not unlike many young men, found his sweetheart at a young age. He was devoted to her, and they both made plans for marriage. However, there was a problem. Matheson became diagnosed with an incurable disease that would eventually ravage his eyes and leave him completely blind. Upon breaking the terrible news to his fiancé, she informed him that she did "not want to be the wife of a blind man." They went their separate ways, and Matheson was understandably devastated. His disease seemed not only to rob him of his sight, but his wife and the future that they would build. It seemed that it would steal away his future education and all of his aspirations.

But the pain and sorrow of that moment produced a song that would be sung and celebrated for centuries. Of writing the song, Matheson said, "I am quite sure that the whole work was completed in five minutes . . . I have no natural gift of rhythm . . . this came like a dayspring from on high. I have never been able to gain once more the same fervor in a verse." While George Matheson was an intelligent and accomplished writer and theologian, he still recognized the ineptitude he had for writing such a brilliant song. He knew that God had done this work through him—that the Holy Spirit was the true author of such poignant words. From Matheson's heartbreak, God brought beauty. God is always making the brokenness of the world into works of art that bring glory to His name.

God can and will bring about goodness from the sufferings that we experience on this earth. Romans 8:28 reminds us of the truth that He works all things together for the good of His beloved. He does not leave brokenness and suffering unattended. Instead, He actively uses them to bring us closer to Himself. This hymn's third stanza reminds us of our imperishable future in Christ, the splendor of that tearless morning that we shall finally meet Christ face to face.

We will all experience suffering and sorrow in differing measures during this lifetime. George Matheson surely did not anticipate blindness or a broken engagement in his future; nevertheless, when these difficulties struck, he submitted himself to the work of God. He made the choice to actively think on excellent and wonderful things. He took to heart Paul's words found in Philippians 4:8 when he reflected on the honorable, just, pure, lovely, commendable, excellent, and praiseworthy things of God. Because of what he filled his mind with, he was able to write those things on paper and lead others in praise of God. May we too choose to think of the glorious things of God, and may they also heap great comfort on our souls.

Questions

Take note of the subjects of each stanza: love, light, joy, and the cross. What does each key phrase point to or symbolize?

Reflect on Romans 8:28 in light of this song. Do you truly trust God to bring about goodness from the brokenness you have experienced?

Read Revelation 21:4. How does this verse give you hope in Christ? In what ways does this truth sustain you amid sorrow?

Holy, Holy, Holy!
Lord God Almighty!

Reginald Heber, ca. 1826

Holy, Holy, Holy! Lord God Almighty!
Early in the morning our song shall rise to thee.
Holy, Holy, Holy! Merciful and mighty!
God in three persons, blessed Trinity!

Holy, Holy, Holy! All the saints adore thee,
casting down their golden crowns around the glassy sea;
cherubim and seraphim falling down before thee,
which wert and art and evermore shalt be.

Holy, Holy, Holy! though the darkness hide thee,
Though the eye made blind by sin thy glory may not see,
only Thou art holy; there is none beside thee,
perfect in pow'r, in love, and purity.

Holy, Holy, Holy! Lord God Almighty!
All thy works shall praise thy name in earth and sky and sea.
Holy, Holy, Holy! Merciful and mighty!
God in three persons, blessed Trinity.

week 1
day 2

READ:
LEVITCUS 19:1-2
I SAMUEL 2:2
REVELATION 4:8-11

Holy, Holy, Holy

The hymn "Holy, Holy, Holy" was penned by Reginald Heber and was born out of a passion for elevating the quality of hymns at the time. Living in the 1700s, Heber saw a need in the church—better artistry in the lyrics of the popular songs. He attended Oxford University where he studied poetry and excelled in the subject. He hoped to use his God-given gifts along with his impressive education to better the church, however he was met with an uphill battle.

Not only did Heber desire to write better lyrics for church worship services, but he went so far as to envision an entirely new hymnal for the church in London—a hymnal that would correspond to the patterns within liturgical churches. This attempt was thwarted by the bishop of London, and he soon found himself in a small, insignificant village. But in this small place he wrote all 57 of his works, "Holy, Holy, Holy" among them. His work was discovered by his wife posthumously, and she went on to publish the work in his honor.

It is strange to think about how something considered so insignificant at the time sends seismic ripples through time and space to impact our culture today. The church that Heber belonged to never saw this hymn come to life, but it is ingrained in our culture centuries later. Perhaps this is because the subject matter of this hymn is so compelling and beautiful. Heber's view of God came through so plainly in the words that he penned—God is holy, good, and worthy of all praise.

Based out of Revelation 4:8-11, this song paints a powerful picture of the thoughts we can look forward to having in eternity. God's holiness is a prevalent and necessary theme throughout the pages of Scripture, yet it is a quality we often forget to acknowledge in our day-to-day life. Not only does His holiness warrant eternal, earnest praise, but it also calls us to respond by pursuing holiness in our own lives. Leviticus 19:1-2 tells us explicitly that God has an expectation upon believers to be holy because of He Himself is holy.

Peter repeats this thought in his first epistle. When we are in Christ, we are given the opportunity to become holy ourselves through the power of the Holy Spirit that dwells within us. Pursuing holiness means changing our lives to hate sin and flee from it, loving others with the same love with which we are loved by God and looking to God as the ultimate and exclusive object of our praise and worship. Thinking and singing about the holiness of God changes us and urges us to leave behind the things of this world and look to Christ instead.

Questions

Read Revelation 4:8-11. How does this passage impact your understanding of who God is?

Meditate on 1 Samuel 2:2. How does this verse shape your knowledge of what idolatry might look like?

Spend some time in prayer, praising God for His holiness and asking God to continually grow your understanding of His holiness so that your relationship with Him would be deepened.

This is My Father's World

Maltbie D. Babcock, ca. 1901

This is my Father's world,
And to my listening ears
All nature sings, and round me rings
The music of the spheres.
This is my Father's world:
I rest me in the thought
Of rocks and trees, of skies and seas--
His hand the wonders wrought.

This is my Father's world:
The birds their carols raise,
The morning light, the lily white,
Declare their Maker's praise.
This is my Father's world:
He shines in all that's fair;
In the rustling grass I hear Him pass,
He speaks to me everywhere.

This is my Father's world:
O let me ne'er forget
That though the wrong seems oft so strong,
God is the Ruler yet.
This is my Father's world:
Why should my heart be sad?
The Lord is King: let the heavens ring!
God reigns; let earth be glad!

week 1
day 3

READ:
GENESIS 1
JOB 38:1-11
2 PETER 3:13

This is My Father's World

Coming from a wealthy family, Maltbie Babcock was afforded a great education. He was heavily involved in music programs while participating in his undergraduate degree, but he eventually went on to complete a theological degree at Auburn Seminary. Being called into vocational ministry, Babcock became the pastor in the city of Lockport, New York.

Enamored by the Great Lakes region's beauty, he was known for often slipping away to hike, run, and enjoy God's creation, famously telling his secretary, "I am going out to see my Father's world." He went on to write out 16 stanzas of poetry, each beginning with the iconic phrase. Thus, the lyrics to a hymn were born.

Ultimately, he pastored a few other churches and often spoke publicly for events at colleges. At the age of 42, his church family would gift him with a trip to Israel, and shortly thereafter he set-off by ship. Unfortunately, he would never see the Holy Land. He contracted a deadly disease and passed away in Naples, Italy. After his untimely death, his wife compiled his writings and poetry, including the words to "This is My Father's World" into a book entitled, "Thoughts for Everyday Living." In 1916, the poem was put to a melody, and Babcock's phrase became immortalized in song.

Babcock so loved nature because he so loved the One who created it all. Not to be confused with worshiping nature, he knew and found the value in admiring the beauty and detail with which God created the world. When he would hike and run through nature, he allowed himself to worship God in a distinct way—he came to know God's character through observing and appreciating the intricacies and beauty of the earth. When we read Genesis 1, we see the magnificence of God's power, that He created all that we see today out of nothing. He spoke it all into existence. He saw that it was all good. So we too should look on at His glory which is displayed in the heavens and earth and see and know that it is good.

In Job's suffering, after crying out to God many times and in many ways, God answered in a whirlwind, reminding His servant of His power and might through describing His own creation. God laid the foundations of the earth, and the stars sang together in joy of God. He shut in the sea, marking the boundaries of the waters. He commanded night and day, and the orbits aligned and obeyed. All the world is His, and He has seen fit to display His wondrous glories through creation. This is our Father's world. When we take the time to observe and admire His hand in the sunsets, animals, and seas, we are allowed and enabled to see God's power, glory, and might.

Questions

Have you felt closer to God by observing nature? In what ways do the Grand Canyon, Niagara Falls, or other iconic landmarks display the glories of God?

In what ways does Job 38:1-11 grow your understanding of God's power? In what ways does this passage change the way that look at creation?

Meditate on 2 Peter 3:13. In light of this passage, how do you think the new heavens and new earth will differ from what we live in now? How does this display the glory of God?

Swing Low, Sweet Chariot

Traditional Spiritual, ca. 1850s

Swing low, sweet chariot
Coming for to carry me home

I looked over Jordan, and what did I see
Coming for to carry me home
A band of angels coming after me
Coming for to carry me home

Swing low, sweet chariot
Coming for to carry me home

If you get there before I do
Coming for to carry me home
Tell all my friends I'm coming, too
Coming for to carry me home

Swing low, sweet chariot
Coming for to carry me home

I'm sometimes up and sometimes down
Coming for to carry me home
But still my soul feels heavenly bound
Coming for to carry me home

Swing low, sweet chariot
Coming for to carry me home

If I get there before you do
Coming for to carry me home
I'll cut a hole and pull you through
Coming for to carry me home

week 1
day 4

READ:
LEVITICUS 25
2 KINGS 2:11-12
1 THESSALONIANS 4:13-18

Swing Low, Sweet Chariot

"Swing Low, Sweet Chariot" is one of the most iconic spiritual songs of our nation. It is authorless, born out of the bleak and wretched time of American slavery. Despite its sorrowful background, this spiritual song hinges on the hope of Jesus Christ. There is no known composer of this song; it survived by being passed orally generation through generation. There was, however, a stunning story of how the song was popularized and formally introduced Americans to the beauty and solemn power in African American spirituals.

Established in 1866, Fisk University is a private, historically black school located in Nashville, Tennessee. The school was wildly successful, bringing in 900 students within a matter of months. But five years into its establishment, the school ran low on funding. In 1871, the university established an a cappella group that was founded for the purpose of fundraising. After a successful performance in Ohio, the singing group was invited to perform at a large church in Brooklyn, New York. Up until this point, the group was nameless. One night, the director prayed, agonizing over what the group of phenomenal singers should be called. The Fisk Jubilee Singers was only fitting; they were named after the year of Jubilee as described in Leviticus 25 in which all debts were canceled and all captives and slaves were freed.

In 1871, the Jubilee singers performed for Plymouth Church located in Brooklyn. The performance was so moving and beautiful that the pastor of Plymouth Church pleaded with his audience to give all of the money in their pockets to Fisk University, and a sum of $1,300 was raised that night. The story of the astounding group of musicians was told worldwide, leading to performance engagements across the globe.

The Jubilee singers made "Swing Low, Sweet Chariot" famous and thereby introduced the world to the persistent faith and hope that is exemplified in African American spirituals. This hymn points believers toward the imperishable hope that we have in Jesus Christ. It is an allusion to Elijah in 2 Kings, who never tasted death but was taken up to heaven by a chariot of fire. It echoes the expectation found in 1 Thessalonians 4:14, that we do not grieve as those who have no hope, "Or if we believe that Jesus died and rose again, in the same way, through Jesus, God will bring with him those who have fallen asleep." For the unknown voices who sang this tune while enslaved, it pointed them toward hope. For the Jubilee Singers who sought out education in their freedom, it pointed them toward hope. We would do well to learn from their voice and cling to the hope of Jesus Christ in both life and death.

Questions

Read Leviticus 25:10. In what ways do you see God's grace, mercy, and forgiveness through His institution of the year of Jubilee in Israel?

Reflect on 1 Thessalonians 4:13-18. What does this passage teach you about the hope that we have in Christ? How is this hope conveyed through the hymn?

Spend some time in prayer, asking that God would grow your hope in Him and give you a better understanding of the importance of hoping in Him.

I Need Thee Every Hour

Annie Sherwood Hawkes, ca. 1872

I need thee every hour,
most gracious Lord;
no tender voice like thine
can peace afford.

I need thee, O I need thee;
every hour I need thee!
O bless me now, my Savior,
I come to thee.

I need thee every hour,
stay thou near by;
temptations lose their power
when thou art nigh.

I need thee every hour,
in joy or pain;
come quickly, and abide,
or life is vain.

I need thee every hour;
teach me thy will,
and thy rich promises
in me fulfill.

week 1
day 5

READ:
PSALM 16:11
2 CORINTHIANS 3:5
PHILIPPIANS 4:19

I Need Thee Every Hour

Annie Sherwood was a talented poet from a young age. She was encouraged in her church by her pastor to continually write, and he would often arrange for music to accompany her poems, creating hymns that their congregation would sing. Annie wrote this song in 1872 when she was 37. Though she felt consumed by her day-to-day tasks as a wife and mother, she was overwhelmed with nearness to the Lord. This song was written in response to those feelings, the words coming to her as she thought upon how blessed it is to be in the presence of the Lord.

Though Annie went on to write 400 more hymns in her lifetime, "I Need Thee Every Hour" was the nearest to her heart. In the coming years when she experienced the death of her husband, she was caused to reflect on the hymn saying, "I did not understand at first why this hymn had touched the great throbbing heart of humanity. It was not until long after, when the shadow fell over my way, the shadow of great loss, that I understood something of the comforting power in the words which I had been permitted to give out to others in my hour of sweet serenity and peace." Annie Sherwood was a woman who knew the high value of the Lord's presence in her life, and through her writing she sought (and succeeded) to draw hearts and minds toward the goodness of the Lord.

Philippians 4:19 is a verse that reminds us that every need that we have is supplied in Jesus Christ. We need Him to provide for us, we need Him for security, we need Him for fellowship, we need Him for life, and we need Him for salvation. He sustains us with every breath and every step. It is impossible to find any sufficiency in this world—all of it comes from God Himself.

Annie wrote this hymn while thinking of those who do not know God, who have not tasted and seen that the Lord is good. When we think upon the words of this hymn and reflect on the immense necessity we have for God, we ought to think about the lost as well. We rejoice in singing this hymn because we have experienced the joy that comes in the salvation of the Lord, but there are still so many who have yet to hear the good news of the gospel. When we examine and recognize our daily need of the Lord, we are caused to remember that we have a responsibility to bear. We must share the gospel. We must tell the lost and dying world around us of the hope and joy in relying on Jesus Christ for eternal, unending salvation.

Questions

Read 2 Corinthians 3:5. What are some ways that you are prone to find sufficiency in yourself rather than in God?

Meditate on Psalm 16:11. How does this verse inform your understanding of needing the Lord's presence in your life?

Spend some time in self-examination and prayer, asking that the Lord would reveal to you the need you have for Him and grow your love of Him.

He sustains us with every breath and every step

WEEK 1

Scripture Memory

We know that all things work together for the good of those who love God, who are called according to his purpose.

ROMANS 8:28

Weekly Reflection

What are some of the ways that your understanding of God's character has been expanded throughout this week?

In what ways did studying these hymns teach you to worship the Lord more fully in all circumstances?

What was your favorite hymn to study this week? Why?

What passage of Scripture stood out to you the most this week? In what ways did it draw you nearer to God?

How can you practically apply what you have learned this week?

Choose a verse or passage from this week's reading to reflect on. How does this verse/passage point your relationship toward Christ?

Just As I Am

Charlotte Elliott, ca. 1835

Just as I am, without one plea,
but that thy blood was shed for me,
and that thou bidd'st me come to thee,
O Lamb of God, I come, I come.

Just as I am, and waiting not
to rid my soul of one dark blot,
to thee, whose blood can cleanse each spot,
O Lamb of God, I come, I come.

Just as I am, though tossed about
with many a conflict, many a doubt,
fightings and fears within, without,
O Lamb of God, I come, I come.

Just as I am, thou wilt receive,
wilt welcome, pardon, cleanse, relieve;
because thy promise I believe,
O Lamb of God, I come, I come.

week 2
day 1

READ:
JOHN 6:37
ROMANS 5:8
TITUS 3:5

Just As I Am

When she was 32, Charlotte Elliott suffered from a debilitating disease that left her disabled. She was a bitter and angry woman, and a minister named Cesar Malan paid her a visit while she was embroiled in frustration at her condition. After a fiery outburst, Malan said to her, "you are tired of yourself, aren't you? You are holding to your hate and anger because you have nothing else in the world to cling to." Charlotte then asked for the cure for such consuming bitterness that she clung to, to which the minster astutely responded, "The faith you are trying to despise."

After this comment, Charlotte became attuned with the message the minister was relaying—there is joy and freedom in the gospel of Jesus Christ. She then asked her new friend what she could do to possess such great joy and peace, and Malan expressed that all she had to do was give herself to God, just as she was.

"I would come to God just as I am? Is that right?" Almost in disbelief at the simplicity, she uttered the phrase that would then become such a powerful song. As she matured in her faith, Charlotte became affectionate toward one particular verse in the Bible, John 6:37, "Everyone the Father gives me will come to me, and the one who comes to me I will never cast out." She forsook the bitterness that consumed her for so much of her life and replaced it with the security and delight that is found in a relationship with Christ, knowing that He would accept her if she would come to Him. Over her lifetime, she continued to write hymns, over 150 in all. She never experienced freedom from her physical ailments, but instead of being encased in the sorrow of her circumstances, she went to Jesus, just as she was, delighting in His joy and peace along the way.

Each of us has the privilege to come to Jesus just as we are. Romans 5:8 reminds us of this truth. While we were still sinners, Christ still died for us. As believers, we have security in Him, knowing that He still loves us in spite of our brokenness and sinfulness. Coming to Him just as we are is the cure for the bitterness and anger in which we indulge ourselves. We do not have to be consumed by being "in the right place" in order to have a relationship with God. We do not have to worry about looking or feeling a certain way or our own actions being sufficient for our salvation. Titus 3:5 explains to us that God has saved us. It was not by our own righteousness nor by our own actions that we received salvation. It was only according to His abundance and sufficient mercy that we are enabled and empowered to come to Jesus, just as we are.

Questions

What things might be keeping you from coming to Christ, just as you are? Pray that God would free you from those pressures.

Meditate on John 6:37. What does this teach you about the security that is found in God?

Read and reflect on Romans 5:8. In light of this hymn and passage, how is your understanding of the love of God grown?

Go, Tell it on the Mountain

Published by John Wesley Work III, ca. 1907

Go, tell it on the mountain,
over the hills and everywhere;
go, tell it on the mountain
that Jesus Christ is born.

While shepherds kept their watching
o'er silent flocks by night,
behold, throughout the heavens
there shone a holy light.

The shepherds feared and trembled
when lo! above the earth
rang out the angel chorus
that hailed our Savior's birth.

Down in a lowly manger
the humble Christ was born,
and God sent us salvation
that blessed Christmas morn.

week 2
day 2

READ:
MATTHEW 28:19
LUKE 2:20
ISAIAH 52:7

Go, Tell it On the Mountain

We typically hear this song in the month of December as we herald in the Christmas season. The lyrics of this hymn are blatant references to the experience of the shepherds as narrated in the book of Luke. The shepherds were told by angels that their Savior had been born, telling them also where to find the babe. Upon this announcement, the skies burst with hosts of angels singing praises to God. The shepherds then find the Messiah, wrapped in swaddling clothes, just as the angel had said. It makes sense that this would grow to be a Christmas carol; it is explicitly about the events in Luke 2. But this song has a rich history, one that you might not expect it to have.

This song, filled with the hope of the nativity, is a song born from the tragic experiences of American slavery. "Go, Tell it on the Mountain" is an African American spiritual. Similar to the history of "Swing Low, Sweet Chariot," this song was made famous because of the Fisk Jubilee Singers. By 1907, many of the African American spirituals had become successful, but "Go, Tell it on the Mountain" had yet to be published formally. John Wesley Work, Jr. was passionate about the preservation of African American spirituals and was eventually able to publish this song formally, thereby cementing in history the words composed by slaves that had only been handed down orally up to this point.

There is an immense amount of hope that can be found in the fact that this song was born out of harsh trials and cruel treatments. The same hope that was possessed by the African American slaves who sang this song in grueling conditions is the same hope that we partake in today. The gospel is powerful enough to transcend dire conditions, beautiful enough to grant abounding comfort to those amid strife, and strong enough to save every soul that calls Jesus Christ "Lord."

Not only does this song point its hearers toward the hope that is in Jesus Christ, but it also compels the listeners to go and tell of the good news themselves. The hope that we personally find in the gospel message is a hope that emboldens us to go out and spread the good news of new life in Jesus with those who have not heard. This song is essentially putting into tune the Great Commission found in the words of Matthew 28:19-20.

We would do well to learn from the mouths that sang this song in centuries past. These were brothers and sisters in Christ who, despite unfathomable circumstances, believed, trusted, and delighted in the hope that is Jesus Christ. When we cause ourselves to think on the pure hope that is only found in Jesus, the natural response is to then go and tell it on the mountains, over the hills and everywhere.

Questions

Read Isaiah 52:7. What are some ways you see this Bible verse reflected in this hymn?

Spend some time in self-examination. Do you find yourself emboldened by the hope of the gospel to go and share it with those around you?

Read Luke 2:20. What are some things we can learn about the shepherd's actions after they saw Mary, Joseph, and Jesus?

Revive Us Again

William P. Mackay, ca. 1863

We praise thee, O God, for the Son of thy love,
For Jesus who died and is now gone above.
Hallelujah, thine the glory!
Hallelujah, Amen!
Hallelujah, thine the glory!
Revive us again.

We praise thee, O God, for thy Spirit of light,
Who has shown us our Savior and scattered our night.
All glory and praise to the Lamb that was slain,
Who has borne all our sins and has cleansed ev'ry stain.
Revive us again - fill each heart with thy love;
May each soul be rekindled with fire from above.

week 2
day 3

READ:

HABAKKUK 3:2

PSALM 80:7

PSALM 85:6

Revive Us Again

William Paton Mackay had the benefit of being raised by a mother who loved the Lord deeply. It is said that she proclaimed the gospel and prayed for him often. Unfortunately, he was never interested in Christianity or in God. He continued on in his life, unbothered by religion, and devoted himself to becoming a doctor.

One day, in his practice of medicine, Mackay encountered a man who was badly injured during work. The circumstances were dire, and Mackay knew that his patient would soon succumb to his wounds. When asking his patient if there were any relatives that could be notified, the man replied that there was no one to tell except for his landlady as he owed her a small debt and wished that she would bring "the book" to him. Mackay continued to care for the man in his dying days and was always struck by his joyful disposition despite facing death.

After the man's passing, Mackay and the nurses were left with the responsibility trying to figure out what to do with the beloved book that the man had found such importance in. The nurse handed off the special book to the doctor who was astonished by what he had just received—this was his Bible. His name was still inscribed on the flyleaf. The Bible that his mother had given him so long ago, the one that he had sold, had found him again. The book that he had practically discarded was the same book that brought solace to a dying man.

Mackay decided to keep the Bible this time. Letting the Word of God transform him, he gave his life to Christ and eventually became a minister. The words of the hymn were born out of a life revived by Jesus Christ, and through this song, Mackay has empowered countless more hearts to let themselves be revived by the Word of God.

We often all need intervention from God to revive our tired and bored hearts. We are imperfect and sinful creatures who can grow bored of the Christian life if we are not stoking the fire of God within our hearts. The hymn is an anthemic song of praise, heralding the Holy Spirit to come set revival on the hearts of each of His people. The weariness of the world is no match for the revitalizing power of the Holy Spirit within us.

The prophet Habakkuk proclaims his knowledge and understanding of God, pleading his case before the Father, that revival would be brought to His people through His work. We are revived at heart when we allow the hand and work of God to transform us. The psalmist, in Psalm 85:6 cries out to God for revival, "that Your people may rejoice in You." When we are a revived people by God, our hearts are led in rejoicing in Him. The revival of our heart is the fixation of our souls on God. When we are revived by Him, we find all the more reason to rejoice in His goodness.

Questions

Read Psalm 85:6. What does it mean to be revived by God and rejoice in Him? Why is this an important thing to understand?

Reflect on some things in your life that you feel the need for God's reviving intervention. Spend some time in prayer, asking that God would redeem and revive those parts of your life.

Meditate on Psalm 80:7, and think about the ways that you have seen God's hand in restoring your life. How does this hymn and this verse encourage you to know the power of the restoring and reviving hand of God?

Jesus Loves the Little Children

C. H. Woolston, ca. 1864
Composed by George F. Root

Jesus calls the children dear,
"Come to me and never fear,
For I love the little children of the world;
I will take you by the hand,
Lead you to the better land,
For I love the little children of the world."

Jesus loves the little children,
All the children of the world.
Red and yellow, black and white,
All are precious in His sight,
Jesus loves the little children of the world.

Jesus is the Shepherd true,
And He'll always stand by you,
For He loves the little children of the world;
He's a Savior great and strong,
And He'll shield you from the wrong,
For He loves the little children of the world.

I am coming, Lord, to Thee,
And Your soldier I will be,
For You love the little children of the world;
And Your cross I'll always bear,
And for You I'll do and dare,
For You love the little children of the world.

week 2
day 4

READ:
LUKE 18:16
JOHN 3:16
GALATIANS 3:28

Jesus Loves the Little Children

When we think about this hymn that most of us probably learned as children, we do not necessarily think that it was written and composed by a musical mastermind. It is a simple tune with simple lyrics that truthfully and purely conveys the basic message of the gospel. It is uncomplicated so that children can not only grasp the concept but also remember the melody. In all of its simplicity lies the methods of a genius. George Fredrick Root was born in Massachusetts in 1820 and by the age of thirteen had already acquired the ability to play thirteen different instruments. He eventually went on to become a music teacher in New York, a church organist, and a composer. Needless to say, he was quite an accomplished musician.

In 1861, when the Civil War broke out, George felt a deep sense of commitment to the Union and devoted his talent to writing songs that would uplift and uphold the soldiers. George understood the power of music and knew that writing songs for the troops was a tangible way that he could boost their morale and serve them. After the war was won, the tune remained popular, but another writer decided to adjust the lyrics into what we now sing. Thus, the song we know and love today originated as a battle cry.

There is something special about the knowledge that soldiers who were giving their lives for justice were comforted by singing a song that would eventually exemplify the love of Christ. This song that we now reserve for teaching to children, is something that once brought great comfort to grown men going into battle. The melody that served the Union and became a ballad for them is now a song that we use to explain the indiscriminate love that God extends to His people.

Remembering such a simple truth is not only essential for children but for adults as well. We all are in need of simple yet sturdy reminders that God loves us dearly and boundlessly. For this same reason, one of the first verses we teach our little ones is John 3:16; it is of the utmost importance that the foundation of our faith is built on the sacrifice of Christ and the incredible love displayed in that act. We are again reminded of this importance in Luke 18:16, when Jesus fearlessly pushed back on the demands of His disciples and let the children come to Him without hindrance. We too are encouraged to come to Christ, regardless of race or gender or status. Jesus Christ does not discriminate who comes to Him, and in the same vein, we should not allow ourselves to pick and choose with whom we share the gospel.

Questions

Read Luke 18:16. What does Jesus's attentiveness to children teach you about His character?

Reflect on Galatians 3:28. How is this verse exemplified in the hymn? Why is it important to understand God as indiscriminate?

Is your understanding of God's love foundational to your faith and relationship with Him? What are some ways that your understanding of God's love impacts your relationship with Him?

Leaning On the Everlasting Arms

Anthony J. Showalter, ca. 1887

What a fellowship, what a joy divine,
leaning on the everlasting arms;
what a blessedness, what a peace is mine,
leaning on the everlasting arms.

Leaning, leaning,
safe and secure from all alarms;
leaning, leaning,
leaning on the everlasting arms.

O how sweet to walk in this pilgrim way,
leaning on the everlasting arms;
O how bright the path grows from day to day,
leaning on the everlasting arms.

What have I to dread, what have I to fear,
leaning on the everlasting arms?
I have blessed peace with my Lord so near,
leaning on the everlasting arms.

week 2 day 5

READ:

DEUTERONOMY 33:27

PROVERBS 3:5

PSALM 71:6

Leaning On the Everlasting Arms

Anthony Showalter was a gifted musician known throughout the South for having written over 130 different music books, and he devoted his talents to the church. As a lover of Gospel music, he was fond of starting singing schools within different churches, and one such church was in Alabama. He was also known for his attention to his students, both present and prior. He was interested in the lives of his students, and it was not uncommon for them to correspond for years after their time in the singing school.

One day, as he was finished with his work, he returned to his home wherein he had received two letters from two of his former students. Those letters contained great tragedy—both young men had the tribulation of losing their wives. Being a wise and caring minster, he sought to pen some words that might uphold and encourage these young men amid their immense griefs. Opening his Bible, he came to Deuteronomy 33:27, "The God of old is your dwelling place, and underneath are the everlasting arms. . ." As he wrote his responses, the refrain of the hymn we know so well came to him. Leaning, leaning, safe and secure from all alarms; leaning, leaning, leaning on the everlasting arms. Finding himself to be unable to write the rest of the lyrics, he enlisted the help of a good friend named Elisha Hoffman. Together they wrote a hymn that still brings solace and encouragement to the downtrodden today.

What great joy to cling to in the midst of great sorrow! God's everlasting arms are forever upholding us, no matter the depth of trial. The truth of Deuteronomy 33:27 still penetrates our hearts today: our God is eternal, He is our dwelling place, and His strength is everlasting. We have abounding hope because of this. He is a God who is all-powerful and mighty, and we can trust in the security offered to us in His everlasting arms. Proverbs 3:5 wisely counsels believers to not lean on the limited understanding of our own minds but to trust in the Lord. Our understanding is futile to lean on, but the Lord's arms are everlasting and strong to support us. The psalmist rightly proclaims, "I have leaned on you from birth; you took me from my mother's womb" (Psalm 71:6). In our most helpless state, as a babe in the womb of our mothers, we leaned on Him. We always have and always will desperately need the Lord. And in our daily desperation, we can have assurance that His everlasting arms will support us lavishly when we choose to lean on Him.

Questions

Reflect on Proverbs 3:5. In what ways are you prone to lean on your own understanding rather than trust in God? Why might this hurt your relationship with God?

Read Psalm 71:6. How does this verse expand your understanding of the depth and breadth of our need for God?

Consider Deuteronomy 33:27 in light of this hymn. What are some ways that you can put into action, "leaning on the everlasting arms"?

God's everlasting arms are forever upholding us, no matter the depth of trial.

WEEK 2

Scripture Memory

There is no Jew or Greek, slave or free, male and female; since you are all one in Christ Jesus.

GALATIANS 3:28

Weekly Reflection

What are some of the ways that your understanding of God's character has been expanded throughout this week?

In what ways did studying these hymns teach you to worship the Lord more fully in all circumstances?

What was your favorite hymn to study this week? Why?

What passage of Scripture stood out to you the most this week? In what ways did it draw you nearer to God?

How can you practically apply what you have learned this week?

Choose a verse or passage from this week's reading to reflect on. How does this verse/passage point your relationship toward Christ?

The Love of God

Frederick M. Lehman, ca. 1917

The love of God is greater far
Than tongue or pen can ever tell;
It goes beyond the highest star,
And reaches to the lowest hell;
The guilty pair, bowed down with care,
God gave His Son to win;
His erring child He reconciled,
And pardoned from his sin.

Oh, love of God, how rich and pure!
How measureless and strong!
It shall forevermore endure—
The saints' and angels' song.

When hoary time shall pass away,
And earthly thrones and kingdoms fall,
When men who here refuse to pray,
On rocks and hills and mountains call,
God's love so sure, shall still endure,
All measureless and strong;
Redeeming grace to Adam's race—
The saints' and angels' song.

Could we with ink the ocean fill,
And were the skies of parchment made,
Were every stalk on earth a quill,
And every man a scribe by trade;
To write the love of God above
Would drain the ocean dry;
Nor could the scroll contain the whole,
Though stretched from sky to sky.

week 3
day 1

READ:

JOHN 3:16

REVELATION 6:15-16

1 JOHN 4:10

The Love of God

Meir Ben Isaac Nehorai was a Jewish poet who lived in Germany during the span of the eleventh century and is often accredited with composing the famous final stanza of "The Love of God." Contained in the poem entitled "Hadamut," the poet interwove the prose about the height, depth, and breadth of God's love for His people. These words would prove to be so powerful that they would more than withstand the tests of time.

After 800 years of being written, these words resurged in an unlikely place—the walls of an asylum. Presumably, after the troubled soul that had inhabited the asylum room had passed away, the workers found the scribbled words on the walls. From there, a legend was born: an individual who suffered extreme mental torment had an intense moment of clarity, of which he used to think on the magnificence of the Lord.

Years later, there was a man named Frederick Lehman, who was struggling to find a third stanza to match two verses of a hymn he had written. Hearing the story of the unknown inmate who wrote the prolific words on his boarding room walls in a sermon, Lehman saw that the words were the perfect complement to the first two verses of his song. His hymn was finished, and it is a song we still enjoy today.

The message of God's love for mankind is central to the gospel message and to the overarching theme of the Bible. 1 John 4:10 reminds us of this by pointing us to the fact that Christ was sent to die to be the propitiation for our sins. The purpose of Christ on the cross was to die in our place, and the purpose of His victorious resurrection was to defeat death so that we might partake in eternal life alongside Him. The power of this hymn resides in the vivid proclamation that God's love for us is astounding, overwhelming, and incomprehensible.

The message is clear: the love of God is rich and pure, cannot be contained within this world, and is perfectly displayed by Jesus's merciful and gracious sacrifice on the cross. We could write this across the skies forever and not exhaust its depth. We could fill every sea with the love of God and still not contain it all. We could sing this hymn forever and still not praise Him as much as He deserves.

The love of God is important in our Christian lives. It compels us to love others with excellence and steers our hearts to be more merciful and gracious, conforming to the likeness of Christ Himself. This hymn calls us to dwell on the love of Christ, and when we allow ourselves to diligently think on Him, our affections are directed heavenward. The love of Christ not only changes our lives and grants us security but calls us to serve others in a radical and revolutionary way.

Questions

Read and reflect on Revelation 6:15-16. In what ways do you see the truth of this verse reflected in this hymn?

Focus on John 3:16. What are some of the ways that this verse teaches you about the depth of the love of God? List the ways below.

Why does the love of Christ change the way we live? How has your love for others grown as a result of experiencing the love of Christ yourself?

All Creatures of Our God and King

St. Francis of Assisi, ca. 1225

All creatures of our God and King,
lift up your voice and with us sing
Alleluia! Alleluia!
Thou burning sun with golden beam,
thou silver moon with softer gleam,
O praise Him, O praise Him!
Alleluia! Alleluia! Alleluia!

Thou rushing wind that art so strong,
ye clouds that sail in heav'n along,
O praise Him! Alleluia!
Thou rising morn, in praise rejoice,
ye lights of ev'ning find a voice!
O praise Him, O praise Him!
Alleluia! Alleluia! Alleluia!

And all ye men of tender heart,
forgiving others, take your part,
O sing ye! Alleluia!
Ye who long pain and sorrow bear,
praise God and on Him cast your care!
O praise Him, O praise Him!
Alleluia! Alleluia! Alleluia!

Let all things their Creator bless
and worship Him in humbleness,
O praise Him! Alleluia!
Praise, praise the Father, praise the Son,
and praise the Spirit, Three in One:
O praise Him, O praise Him!
Alleluia! Alleluia! Alleluia!

week 3
day 2

READ:
JOB 12:7-10
PSALM 148
LUKE 19:40

All Creatures of Our God and King

Saint Francis of Assisi is a rather legendary Christian figure who is known for his love of nature and animals. He grew up in an affluent family, and when he came to accept Christ, he denounced the indulgences of wealth and began a life of traveling and evangelizing those whom he encountered. He is a prolific figure, and at times it can be difficult to tell which tales are tall and which are true. Nevertheless, there are a myriad of stories that emphasize St. Francis's interaction and tenderness toward creation, showing how he faithfully worshiped God by attending to the creatures in his path.

He is said to have saved a village that was ravaged by a lone wolf by rebuking the creature and commanding it to stop, and it did. There is as tale of a bird perching on his finger, with the saint remaining so still that the bird built her nest there and raised her chicks. Perhaps most famously of all, he is said to have preached a sermon to a flock of birds.

On a hike, he encountered the flock and was surprised that they did not immediately vacate the area. He then decided to remind them of the love of God by saying to them, "My brother and sister birds, you should praise your Creator and always love Him. He gave you feathers for clothes, wings to fly, and all the other things you need." The story goes on that the birds set off for the skies, rejoicing as they went. Just before his death, St. Francis wrote the poem that would eventually turn into "All Creatures of our God and King" after a life well-lived and spent stewarding creation to the glory of God.

This hymn is heavily inspired by the words of Psalm 148. We are creatures bound to worship the Lord, surrounded by a creation that heralds the glories of our Maker. Luke 19:40 reminds us that should we remain silent about the goodness of God, the rocks will cry out. We are not worship-optional beings. God deserves to hear our praises to Him unceasingly. We would do well to think on the sermon that Saint Francis preached to the birds—God is worthy of our praise and our affection, He is our sole provider in this world. We would also do well to follow in the examples of the fowls, rejoicing with gladness to our Creator and Sustainer. If the rocks, birds, sun, moon, and mountains can cry out in praise to the Lord, how much more should we be praising Him as the ones made in His image?

Questions

Read Psalm 148 in its entirety. How does this psalm spur you on to worship the Lord more fully?

Meditate on Job 12:7-10. In what ways does the creation and nature around you teach you about the character of God?

Spend some time in self-examination. Does your worship of God remain steadfast?

I Surrender All

Judson W. Van De Venter, ca. 1896

All to Jesus I surrender,
All to Him I freely give;
I will ever love and trust Him,
In His presence daily live.

I surrender all, I surrender all;
All to Thee, my blessed Savior,
I surrender all.

All to Jesus I surrender,
Make me, Savior, wholly Thine;
Let me feel Thy Holy Spirit,
Truly know that Thou art mine.

All to Jesus I surrender,
Lord, I give myself to Thee;
Fill me with Thy love and power,
Let Thy blessing fall on me.

week 3
day 3

READ:

MATTHEW 19:21

LUKE 18:28-30

ACTS 2:42-47

I Surrender All

The subject of surrendering is prevalent in the Christian life, and not many other hymns speak of the freedoms found in the act of surrendering ourselves to Christ. Judson W. Van De Venter composed this hymn in 1896, and it is still commonly heard in churches today as part of the invitation or altar call of the service. Judson's surrender was a very personal one, though, and his testimony has borne witness through song to many generations that came after him.

Judson had always had a knack for the arts, so it seemed to be a natural fit for him to become an art teacher in his adulthood. He loved music and was an active layperson in his local church. The counsel of friends and family urged him to commit to ministry full time, but it took him five years to fully give himself to the ministry that God had given him. He is quoted as saying, "Lord, if you want me to give my full time to Thy work, I'll do it, I surrender all to Thee." It was this life experience that eventually led him to write the hymn "I Surrender All."

Judson continued to surrender all to Christ throughout the rest of his life, continuing on in various ministries both domestically and globally. His testimony through this song is still a powerful instruction on which believers at every stage need to hear and meditate. Jesus Christ calls upon His people to surrender themselves to Him, and we see this in the example of His twelve disciples. In Luke 18:28-30, Jesus promises His disciples that those who sacrifice their earthly comforts will receive much in heaven. When we forsake earthly pleasures and comforts, we subsequently store up our treasures in heaven. And we do not do this for the love of a fancy crown in heaven; we do this because our ultimate joy and delight is found in God.

There is no shortage of Scriptural references of surrendering what we have for the sake of the Lord and His church. Another example of this precept is in Acts 2:42-47. In this passage, we see that there is a correlation between the fellowship of believers and the exuberant giving of ourselves and our belongings. The early church dedicated themselves to teaching and fellowship, and where teaching and fellowship intersect is where surrender of earthly things is found. We surrender all to Jesus, and when we do so, we often end up caring for the Church as well.

Questions

Read Matthew 19:16-21. What does Jesus's response to the rich, young man tell you about the treasures of this earth as compared to the treasures in heaven?

Meditate on Acts 2:42-47. How does this verse show you tangible ways to surrender and care for those around you?

Spend some time in self-examination. Is there anything that God has been challenging you to surrender? What are some practical steps you can take to more actively surrender yourself to obedience in the Lord?

Doxology

Thomas Ken, ca. 1674

Praise God,
from whom all blessings flow;
Praise Him,
all creatures here below;
Praise Him above,
ye heav'nly host;
Praise Father,
Son, and Holy Ghost.
Amen.

week 3
day 4

READ:
PSALM 150
EPHESIANS 5:19-20
JUDE 1:24-25

Doxology

Born in the greater-London area, Thomas Ken was orphaned at a young age and found himself raised by his half-sister who enrolled him in an all-boys school. His education prepared him intellectually, and his love for the church continued to grow. From there, he went on to become a chaplain and serve at that same school that he had attended years prior.

Hymns were not common at this point in history, and most of the songs that were sung in corporate worship were psalms set to music. In an effort to cultivate a devotional habit among the boys at his school, he began to write hymns which were encouraged to be sung at three distinct points in the day. In 1674, Ken formally published the hymns that he had composed, and the "Doxology" has remained a prominent song in worship services ever since.

This song was not born out of sorrow or heartache but came about because Thomas Ken saw the need to sing devotionally unto the Lord. This song is simple, easy to remember, and conveys a well of profound theological truth about God. He created this song to be sung at the midnight hour if you were unable to fall asleep. He taught the boys under his instruction that if they could not seem to sleep, that there was value in stewarding that time to sing. Instead of being caught up in the emptiness of the night, these boys were caught up in the glory of God. There is something beautiful about a restlessness that gives way to singing praises to our Triune God.

In Ephesians 5:19-20, Paul exhorts the church on the importance of singing and doing so to one another. There is value in reminding one another of God's goodness through the avenue of music. The entire book of Psalms is a testament to the importance of song in our worship of the Lord. King David spent a good portion of his lifetime devoted to singing praises to God and writing them down for all of Israel to sing together.

In the same ways, we should be singing songs to the Lord often as a sign of our devotion to Him and in praise of His good character. In doing so, we have the privilege and opportunity to remind other believers of His praiseworthiness. When we sing about the character of God, we are reminding ourselves of truth that He is worthy of our praise, that He has made a covenant with us, and that He will not forsake us. That lifts our spirits heavenward and grows the God-given joys in our hearts.

Questions

Read Jude 1:24-25. What do these verses show you about the character of God?

Spend some time in Psalm 150. What are some ideas that you see in this passage that are reflected in this hymn?

Take a moment to read and repeat the words of this hymn out loud, praising God for His good character and His faithfulness in your life.

More Love to Thee, O Christ

Elizabeth Prentice, ca. 1856

More love to Thee, O Christ,
More love to Thee!
Hear Thou the prayer I make
On bended knee;
This is my earnest plea:
More love, O Christ, to Thee,
More love to Thee,
More love to Thee!

Once earthly joy I craved,
Sought peace and rest;
Now Thee alone I seek,
Give what is best;
This all my prayer shall be:
More love, O Christ, to Thee,
More love to Thee,
More love to Thee!

Then shall my latest breath
Whisper Thy praise;
This be the parting cry
My heart shall raise;
This still its prayer shall be:
More love, O Christ, to Thee,
More love to Thee,
More love to Thee!

week 3
day 5

READ:

DEUTERONOMY 6:5

PSALM 119:71

ROMANS 8:28

More Love to Thee, O Christ

The frailty of life was an idea that Elizabeth Prentiss was well acquainted with. Considered an invalid, she was very physically limited in her abilities. However, she stewarded this sickness by involving herself heavily in poetry and writing. In 1845 she married a Presbyterian minister who would eventually teach at Union Theological Seminary. All the while, her audience for writing increased, and she published two books that had become best sellers.

Already riddled with insomnia and chronic pain, she experienced the loss of her two children. These events led her to be overwhelmed with anxiety as her health continued to decline. In this period of despair, she found herself very fond of the hymn "Nearer my God, To Thee" which serves as the musical inspiration for "More Love to Thee, O Christ." Of her physical limitations that influenced the writing of this hymn she is quoted as saying, "I see now that to live for God, whether one is allowed the ability to be actively useful or not, is a great thing, and that it is a wonderful mercy to be allowed even to suffer, if thereby one can glorify Him." God used this hymn in spite of her physical limitations and earthly sufferings to receive glory by way of her faithfulness.

Psalm 119:71 says, "It is good for me that I was afflicted, that I might learn your statutes." Prentiss certainly experienced the truth of this verse throughout her life. God, in His goodness and faithfulness to us, teaches us through our pains and disappointments. He doesn't waste our suffering but uses it to bring about growth in our lives. Romans 8:28 confirms this truth, reminding believers that God is attentive and at work in all of our circumstances, bringing about our good and receiving glory from it all.

It is a difficult mindset to acquire in which we see and experience the faithfulness of God through our own difficult circumstances. This hymn helps to empower its listeners to love God increasingly and acknowledging in our prayers that God is the author of goodness, and that we will not want when we are delighted in Him. Through the sorrows and limitations she experienced in her life, Elizabeth Prentiss sought to love God better and glorify Him by remaining obedient to the tasks he had placed before her. This example leads us to examine ourselves—are we living lives that are wholly obedient to the Lord's plan for us?

Questions

What are some ways that God has taught and instructed you because of affliction that you have experienced?

Read and meditate on Deuteronomy 6:5. How does this verse encourage you to give more love to God?

Reflect on Romans 8:28. Do you trust that the Lord is actively at work in all of your experiences to bring about goodness?

God is attentive and at work in all of our circumstances, bringing about our good and receiving glory from it all.

WEEK 3

Scripture Memory

The life of every living thing is in his hand, as well as the breath of all mankind.

JOB 12:10

Weekly Reflection

What are some of the ways that your understanding of God's character has been expanded throughout this week?

In what ways did studying these hymns teach you to worship the Lord more fully in all circumstances?

What was your favorite hymn to study this week? Why?

What passage of Scripture stood out to you the most this week? In what ways did it draw you nearer to God?

How can you practically apply what you have learned this week?

Choose a verse or passage from this week's reading to reflect on. How does this verse/passage point your relationship toward Christ?

There is a Balm in Gilead

African American Spiritual, ca. 1800s

There is a balm in Gilead
to make the wounded whole,
there is a balm in Gilead
to heal the sin-sick soul.

Sometimes I feel discouraged
and think my work's in vain,
but then the Holy Spirit
revives my soul again.

If you cannot preach like Peter,
if you cannot pray like Paul,
you can tell the love of Jesus
and say, "He died for all."

week 4
day 1

READ:
JEREMIAH 8:22
LUKE 4:16-21
1 PETER 2:24

There is a Balm in Gilead

One interesting and unique aspects of African American spirituals is that in many cases, we do not have access to the original melodies. "There is a Balm in Gilead" is one such anomaly. The words of the beautiful spiritual have survived the tragedies of American slavery and the accompanying sorrows, but there are many different interpretations to what the melody is. For this reason, there are differing arrangements depending on whether the performance of this song is a full choir, a single singer, or a whole congregation.

Like many of the spiritual songs that are known today, "There is a Balm of Gilead" has no known composer but was instead passed down orally through generations of those in slavery prior to the Civil War. While we do not have a formal history or story behind this song, we know very well what circumstances produced this powerful prose.

Amid the intense strife of slavery, those who originally sang this song decided not to sing out of anger. Instead, they chose to sing of the promise that Jesus is our healer. Rather than dwelling on the hopeless nature of being enslaved, they chose to sing praises to God, reminding themselves that the Holy Spirit brings restoration of the soul.

The premise of the song is based on Jeremiah 8:22 which says, "Is there no balm in Gilead? Is there no physician there? So why has the healing of my dead people not come about?" This hymn pays homage to this verse by answering the question of where healing can be found: the balm of Gilead is Jesus Christ. Throughout the four Gospels, we see many instances in which Jesus heals those who are broken and hurting around Him. Luke 4:18 is a specific instance in which Jesus reveals that He is the fulfillment of Isaiah's prophecy; He is the One who would give freedom to the captives and oppressed, heal the blind, and bring good news. The slaves who sang with whole hearts of the Balm of Gilead were fixating their eyes on the One who brings hope and liberation and healing—Jesus Christ, the Messiah.

However, it is easy to find ourselves forgetting that all of our healing and freedom in found in Jesus alone. It is easy to run to the things of this world instead of running to heavenly things. We often would rather run to social media than to our Bibles. We would rather speak to friends than pray. We would prefer to sit in our anger and sorrow instead of praising God for His goodness and His faithfulness to liberate us. But when we run to Jesus first, we find healing. When we delight in His Word, we find freedom. When we sing praises to Him, we revel in the hope that only He can provide.

Questions

Read 1 Peter 2:24. How does this verse help you to understand Jesus as the "Balm of Gilead."

Spend some time reflecting on Luke 4:16-21. How does Jesus's fulfillment of the prophecy help you understand the liberation that can be found in Him?

Reflect on the second stanza of the hymn. What are some of the ways the Holy Spirit has faithfully revived your soul?

O How I Love Jesus

Frederick Whitfield, ca. 1855

There is a name I love to hear,
I love to sing its worth;
it sounds like music in my ear,
the sweetest name on earth.

O how I love Jesus,
O how I love Jesus,
O how I love Jesus,
because he first loved me!

It tells me of a Savior's love,
who died to set me free;
it tells me of his precious blood,
the sinner's perfect plea.

It tells of one whose loving heart
can feel my deepest woe;
who in each sorrow bears a part
that none can bear below.

week 4
day 2

READ:

ROMANS 5:8

I PETER 1:8

I JOHN 4:19

O How I Love Jesus

The author of this hymn "O How I Love Jesus" was no stranger to writing. In fact, Frederick Whitfield had published thirty books of poetry during his lifetime. Whitfield was born in a small town in England in 1829 and was fortunate to have a good education garnered from Trinity College in Dublin, Ireland. He would eventually become an ordained minister, but nevertheless he is primarily known for the sweet, uplifting tune of "O How I Love Jesus."

The chorus of this hymn is actually and old American song that has veiled origins. The full hymn as we hear it today is actually a medley of the well-known chorus with one of Whitfield's personal compositions, "There is a Name I love to Hear." Though the final product of the hymn is two separate songs welded together, we would never guess it. These two songs seem to be made for one another, destined to be one full song together.

Part of the appeal of this hymn and the reason this song has been so long-lasting is due to its simplistic nature. It is easy to remember, and it conveys powerful truth to us of which we daily need to be reminded. "O How I love Jesus" is a song that points us toward the great love of Jesus Christ displayed in His sacrifice on the cross, who loved us while we were still sinners (Romans 5:8). This precept is absolutely foundational to our faith, yet it is despicably easy to forget how good it is to think on the great love of God, displayed through Jesus's death, burial, and resurrection.

1 John 4:19 is concise and strong: "We love because He first loved us." All of the love that we can give to God and to our fellow man is an overflow of the love with which Jesus Christ has loved us. His love is what moves us forward. His love is what warrants our love for others. His love is what provides the strength for us to love our enemies and those who persecute us.

1 Peter 1:8 reminds us that we love God though we cannot see Him and have never before seen Him incarnate. We believe in Him and rejoice in His glory because of His love, because we have experienced the evidence of His love in our salvation and receiving the Holy Spirit. God's love changes us—it makes us more like Him. When we sing songs about the love of Jesus, our eyes are refocused on what is good, gracious, and true. When we praise God, and in so doing remember the great love displayed on the cross, we become rejuvenated and refreshed. All of our strength comes from relying on the love Jesus Christ has for us. "O, How I Love Jesus" is an ode to that fact.

Questions

Meditate on Romans 5:8. How does this verse expand your understanding of the love that Jesus has for us?

Read 1 Peter 1:8. In what ways does this verse encourage you to praise God because of the evidence of His love for us?

Spend some time in prayer, asking God to reveal His love to you more fully and teach you how to love Him more.

Praise to the Lord, the Almighty

Joachim Neander, ca. 1680

Praise to the Lord, the Almighty, the King of creation!
O my soul, praise him, for he is your health and salvation!
Come, all who hear; now to his temple draw near,
join me in glad adoration.

Praise to the Lord, above all things so wondrously reigning;
sheltering you under his wings, and so gently sustaining!
Have you not seen all that is needful has been
sent by his gracious ordaining?

Praise to the Lord, who will prosper your work and defend you;
surely his goodness and mercy shall daily attend you.
Ponder anew what the Almighty can do,
if with his love he befriends you.

Praise to the Lord! O let all that is in me adore him!
All that has life and breath, come now with praises before him.
Let the Amen sound from his people again;
gladly forever adore him.

week 4
day 3

READ:

JOB 38:4

1 CHRONICLES 29:10-14

1 THESSALONIANS 5:16-18

Praise to the Lord, the Almighty

Despite being born into a lineage of preachers, Joachim Neander spent his youth in rebellion. Known for being a wild and reckless individual, he joined a group of friends to heckle a local church service one night. However, his intentions were thwarted by the power of the gospel, and upon the reverend's leading, he would come to know the Lord and His good gospel. Neander went on to become a clergyman himself at that very church.

He was known for going on walks through a nearby river gorge and thinking of new songs and hymns. However, "Praise to the Lord the Almighty" was composed in much more dire circumstances. While Neander battled tuberculosis, he penned the famous words, "Praise ye the Lord, the Almighty, the King of Creation. O my soul praise Him, for He is thy health and salvation." Can you imagine being on your deathbed and these be the words you choose to sing? Neander is a great example to which we can look of great faithfulness in praising God, rejoicing in all of our circumstances.

1 Thessalonians 5:16-18 exhorts believers to rejoice in God and give thanks to Him in all of our circumstances. Whether we are sick or healthy, poor or wealthy, happy or sad, we always have ample reason to rejoice in God's goodness and good character. This hymn focuses on singing the truth about who God is, teaching us to praise God because He is our King, our defender, and our shelter. For all of these reasons, and so many more, we should gladly adore the Lord.

There is something quite special about this hymn; it is incredibly communal in nature. "Join me in glad adoration." "Have you not seen all that is needful has been sent by his gracious ordaining?" "Let the Amen sound from his people again; gladly forever adore him." All of these phrases from the song are an interaction between believers—they are singing to one another about the worthiness of the Lord to be praised. This hymn is recognizing the crucial tenant of congregational, communal singing. We lift our voices together unto the Lord. We sing His praises together. We sing them to one another to remind our brothers and sisters of His goodness.

After receiving many gifts and offerings for the house of the Lord, David rejoices in God in 2 Chronicles 29:10-14. Like King David, we must choose to remind ourselves of who God is and what He has done for us, no matter what our circumstances might look like. And also, like the hymn, we have a great deal of influence over our brothers and sisters in Christ, encouraging and exhorting them to praise the Lord alongside us.

Questions

Read Job 38:4. In what ways does this verse relate to the hymn in speaking to the worthiness of the Lord to be praised?

Meditate on 1 Thessalonians 5:16-18. What are some ways that you are prone to forsake rejoicing in the Lord? What are some practical ways that you can become someone who is more readied to give thanks to God in all circumstances?

Why do you think it is important to sing communally? List the ways below.

We always have ample reason to rejoice in God's goodness and good character.

WEEK 4

Scripture Memory

Yours, Lord, is the
greatness and the
power and the glory
and the splendor and
the majesty for everything
in the heavens and on
earth belong to You.
Yours, Lord, is the kingdom,
and you are exalted
as head over all.

I CHRONICLES 29:11

Weekly Reflection

What are some of the ways that your understanding of God's character has been expanded throughout this week?

In what ways did studying these hymns teach you to worship the Lord more fully in all circumstances?

What was your favorite hymn to study this week? Why?

What passage of Scripture stood out to you the most this week? In what ways did it draw you nearer to God?

How can you practically apply what you have learned this week?

Choose a verse or passage from this week's reading to reflect on. How does this verse/passage point your relationship toward Christ?

What is the Gospel?

THANK YOU FOR READING AND ENJOYING THIS STUDY WITH US! WE ARE ABUNDANTLY GRATEFUL FOR THE WORD OF GOD, THE INSTRUCTION WE GLEAN FROM IT, AND THE EVER-GROWING UNDERSTANDING IT PROVIDES FOR US OF GOD'S CHARACTER. WE ARE ALSO THANKFUL THAT SCRIPTURE CONTINUALLY POINTS TO ONE THING IN INNUMERABLE WAYS: THE GOSPEL.

We remember our brokenness when we read about the fall of Adam and Eve in the garden of Eden (Genesis 3), where sin entered into a perfect world and maimed it. We remember the necessity that something innocent must die to pay for our sin when we read about the atoning sacrifices in the Old Testament. We read that we have all sinned and fallen short of the glory of God (Romans 3:23) and that the penalty for our brokenness, the wages of our sin, is death (Romans 6:23). We all need grace and mercy, but most importantly, we all need a Savior.

We consider the goodness of God when we realize that He did not plan to leave us in this dire state. We see His promise to buy us back from the clutches of sin and death in Genesis 3:15. And we see that promise accomplished with Jesus Christ on the cross. Jesus Christ knew no sin yet became sin so that we might become righteous through His sacrifice (2 Corinthians 5:21). Jesus was tempted in every way that we are and lived sinlessly. He was reviled yet still yielded Himself for our sake, that we may have life abundant in Him. Jesus lived the perfect life that we could not live and died the death that we deserved.

The gospel is profound yet simple. There are many mysteries in it that we will never understand this side of heaven, but there is still overwhelming weight to its implications in this life. The gospel tells of our sinfulness and God's goodness and a gracious gift that compels a response. We are saved by grace through faith, which means that we rest with faith in the grace that Jesus Christ displayed on the cross (Ephesians 2:8-9). We cannot save ourselves from our brokenness or do any amount of good works to merit God's favor. Still, we can have faith that what Jesus accomplished in His death, burial, and resurrection was more than enough for our salvation and our eternal delight. When we accept God, we are commanded to die to ourselves and our sinful desires and live a life worthy of the calling we have received (Ephesians 4:1). The gospel compels us to be sanctified, and in so doing, we are conformed to the likeness of Christ Himself. This is hope. This is redemption. This is the gospel.

SCRIPTURES TO REFERENCE:

GENESIS 3:15	*I will put hostility between you and the woman, and between your offspring and her offspring. He will strike your head, and you will strike his heel.*
ROMANS 3:23	*For all have sinned and fall short of the glory of God.*
ROMANS 6:23	*For the wages of sin is death, but the gift of God is eternal life in Christ Jesus our Lord.*
2 CORINTHIANS 5:21	*He made the one who did not know sin to be sin for us, so that in him we might become the righteousness of God.*
EPHESIANS 2:8-9	*For you are saved by grace through faith, and this is not from yourselves; it is God's gift—not from works, so that no one can boast.*
EPHESIANS 4:1-3	*Therefore I, the prisoner in the Lord, urge you to walk worthy of the calling you have received, with all humility and gentleness, with patience, bearing with one another in love, making every effort to keep the unity of the Spirit through the bond of peace.*

Thank You

for studying God's Word with us

CONNECT WITH US

@THEDAILYGRACECO

@DAILYGRACEPODCAST

CONTACT US

INFO@THEDAILYGRACECO.COM

SHARE

#THEDAILYGRACECO

VISIT US ONLINE

THEDAILYGRACECO.COM

MORE DAILY GRACE!

THE DAILY GRACE APP

DAILY GRACE PODCAST